MW01254783

City
Without
Altar

Copyright © 2022 Jasminne Mendez
ISBN: 978-1-934819-15-9

Book Cover Art: Elia Alba, *Ivan Study #4*, 2019, photo transfers on fabric, silk
flowers. Courtesy of the artist.
Book Cover Design: Jeffrey Pethybridge
Book Interior Design: Sarah Gzemski

Published by Noemi Press, Inc. A Nonprofit Literary Organization.
www.noemipress.org.

City Without Altar

Jasminne Mendez

Tonight, in this city without altar I hope the dead souls can
see my eyes and turn my watchful gaze into the flicker of a candle flame.

— Lio Xiabo "Fifteen Years of Darkness"

I wish / maps would be without / borders & that we belonged / to no one
& to everyone / at once, what a world that / would be.
    —Yesenia Montilla "Maps"

For my grandparents/Para mis abuelos –
Melva "Mama" Duran, Angel de Jesus "Papito" Duran, Basilia Sosa,
Tomas del Rosario

&

For the victims, survivors and living ancestors of the Haitian Massacre

TABLE OF CONTENTS

III

I

Inheritance

What will they make us forget?

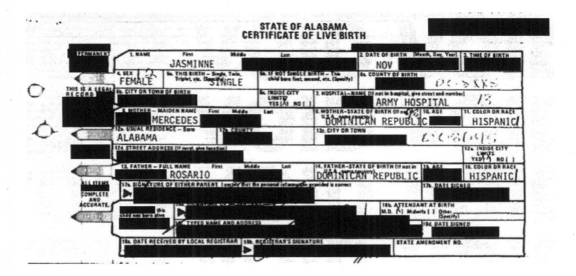

On this day in history. I am born. Alive. Let the record show. I am. Hispanic. Not Black. This is legal. A record. Permanent. All items listed are accurate. And complete. On this day in history. I am. Blacked-out.

What do we inherit and how
do we carry it in the body?

cellular memory
behind my bellybutton a baby
whose heartbeat was never found
whose smile never swam inside
an ultrasound hum the throat swallowed
before it became breath

Who decides what we carry?

In a kitchen on the Southwest side of Houston
       before my daughter is born, I wash white
              rice with Mami, her brown knuckle knocks

my wrist, my baby girl kicks, I palm
       the bulge, my belly, Mami's hand
              rests on mine. *Estas bien?* She asks. I reply,

Are you sure we're not Haitian?
              Her hand recoils like a question mark, *Why*
                    do you want to know?

Because there is this tumor
       this doubt in my mothering
              and I need to cut it out.

How long must we hold on
to what isn't ours?

Abuela rarely smiled
except that one time she held a baby
and we caught it
on camera the first grandson
slept in her ebony
arms painted nails glistened silver
sunlight on a ripple of water
she fed the baby
boy a bottle of breast milk

Her hands shipwrecked and shackled
by Trujillo, heartbreak and hunger I search
her milky eyes for two sons
dead in infancy

she has no pictures of their bones
the one thing we have in common
10,000 sunken slave ships rest
at the bottom of her throat unable to speak
their names
she hurricanes instead

What will we remember?

One day my daughter will tell her daughter
      "we were Black once"

and I hope that unlike me she will shake
      our stories free from the soil

and I hope that unlike me she will reach
      into the back of her mother's throat

and dig until she finds salt or a song she can take
      with her wherever she goes

Where do we go, if we have no record
of where we have been?

I return to water open
my hands a map I point to
where my mothers have been
where I long to go
a lifeline that could be a river
or a border scratch
the blaze of sun off
the back of my neck black
behind the ears it whispers
wake up, wake up
you are from here

II

City Without Altar

Time: 1937

Place: Dajabón, Dominican Republic

Characters:

<u>Madame Telsaint:</u> Haitian woman. A healer. An old woman with old bones. She is water.

<u>Irelia:</u> Dominican-Haitian girl. Young. The fastest runner in Dajabón. She is moon.

<u>Cenalia:</u> Haitian woman. A mother. A wife. She dreams of holding and being held. She is earth.

<u>Cameron:</u> Haitian boy. A brother. He sings like an angel. He is wind.

<u>Me:</u> Dominican-American girl/woman. A witness. She is in pain. She is memory. She is time.

<u>Machete/Surgeon:</u> A machete. A man. He cuts down. He is metal.

<u>Soldier:</u> Dominican man. Wields the machete. Obedient. He is clay.*

* *Machete/Surgeon and Dominican Soldier should be played by same actor*

14

DRAMATURGICAL NOTES

1.   In October of 1937, Dominican dictator Rafael L. Trujillo ordered the mass genocide of Haitians along the northwestern border of the island. At a dance in the city of Dajabón he spoke the following words:

> *For some months, I have traveled and traversed the border in every sense of the word. I have seen, investigated, and inquired about the needs of the population. To the Dominicans who were complaining of the depredations by Haitians living among them, thefts of cattle, provisions, fruits, etc., and were thus prevented from enjoying in peace the products of their labor, I have responded, 'I will fix this.' And we have already begun to remedy the situation. Three hundred Haitians are now dead in Bánica. This remedy will continue.*
>
> *—Rafael L. Trujillo*
> *October 2, 1937*

-as in-

2.   Trujillo wanted to "cleanse the island" of Haitians. Trujillo believed Haitians were a disease--racially and culturally inferior.

3.   *…there are numerous characters which distinguish the negro from other races… Most of these characters tend to confirm the lowly status of the negro in the scale of human evolution.*[1]

-as in -

4.   Trujillo was ¼ Haitian himself.

[1]Mata, Rudolph. *The Surgical Peculiarities of the American Negro.* 1896.

5.   *Out of the swamp the cane appears/to haunt us, and we cut it down.*[2]

                          -as in-

6.   Machete (n.)
     origin from the Spanish - diminutive form of the word macho as in man as in male as in aggressive;

                          -as in-

     a broad blade used for reaping and/or revolution *e.g., The machete was the weapon Trujillo ordered his men to use during the 1937 Haitian massacre;*

                          -as in-

7.   *It isn't easy to look at a machete wound. A machete is nothing but a butcher's cleaver with a slightly longer blade.*[3]

[2]Dove, Rita. "Parsley." *Museum.* 1983.
[3]*Reynolds. Quentin. Murder in the Tropics. Collier's.* 1938.

8.   The 1937 massacre goes by several names: el corte
     "the cutting," or kout kouto-a "the stabbing" and the
     Parsley Massacre.

                          -as in -

9.   Perejil (n.)
     a biennial plant with white flowers and aromatic
     leaves that are crinkly or flat and used as herb
     or to garnish food
     e.g., *Because of the massacre I refuse to cook with
     parsley;*

                          -as in-

     the shibboleth or word used during the massacre
     to determine who was Haitian and who was Dominican
     e.g., *El General has found his word: perejil. /
     Who says it, lives. He laughs, teeth shining /
     out of the swamp.*[4]

---

[4] Dove, Rita. "Parsley." *Museum*. 1983.

10. Trujillo is also remembered by many names: El General /El Jefe/El Chivo.

-as in-

11. The island of Hispaniola is lush with tropical forests and wild animals like goats and pigs. Hills. Lakes. Sugar cane. Rivers and ravines.

-as in-

12. *...the negro in his native African wilds can undergo the most painful operations with apparent indifference...as regards pain the negro of to-day is true to the traditions of his savage ancestors.*[5]

---

[5]Mata, Rudolph. *The Surgical Peculiarities of the American Negro.* 1896.

13. In the city of Dabajón, where most of the killings took place, there is a river. This river is a border. The river is known by many names: Dajabón River, el río Masacre, Massacre River.

-as in -

14. After the cutting, bodies that were not buried in shallow graves were thrown in the river.

-as in-

15. *On account of this blunt sensibility of the nervous system the negro bears surgical operations remarkably well…this makes the negro a most favorable subject for all kinds of surgical treatment with or without preliminary anesthesia.*[6]

---

[6]Mata, Rudolph. *The Surgical Peculiarities of the American Negro.* 1896.

16. Blackout (n.) –
a   transient   dulling   or   loss   of   vision,
consciousness, or memory
e.g., *Some victims of the massacre will blackout*
after they are cut;

-as in-

suppression of information, especially one imposed
on the media by the government
e.g., *Trujillo issued a blackout on information*
released about the massacre.

-as in-

a poem created by blacking out the text of another
document e.g.,

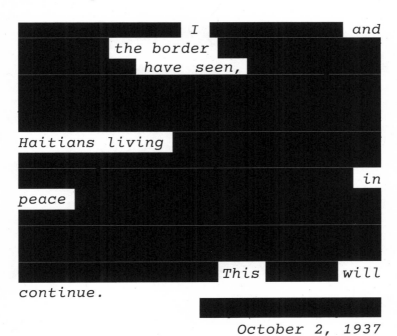

-as in-

a moment in theatre when stage lights are turned off to separate scenes in a play
e.g., There will be many blackouts in this play.

-as in-

17. To this day there is no memorial or marker on either side of the border that lists the names of the victims of the massacre.

-as in-

18. *Misery won't touch you gentle. It always leaves its thumbprints on you; sometimes it leaves them for others to see, sometimes for nobody but you to know of.*[7]

[7]Danticat, Edwidge. *The Farming of Bones*. Soho Press, 2014.

19.   A map of the island.

-as in-

20. All roads lead to

                                    1

                                           2

                                             3

                             4

                                           5

                                         6

                        7

                           8

                                        9

                          10

24

¹*the border.* ²*In the north, the border is the Dajabón River (El Rio Masacre). We used to live in the north. But we went south. Like the river. The river flows straight and through a laguna.* ³*The river becomes el Río Capatillo /Bernard. Maybe once we were Haitian. But we and the border proceeded overland. And we became Dominican. The border runs west. We also ran west. Across the ocean west. So far west I'm not from here or there.* ⁴*The border turns sharply south-east until it reaches the Libón River. The river reaches a road. I am a fork in the road. Half of me here. Half of me there. The border follows this road through the mountains.* ⁵*The mountains meet the Artibonite River. The river runs south-west and merges with another river.* ⁶*The Macasía River. The river runs east.* ⁷*The border runs parallel with the Etang Saumâtre lake. The border curves around the lake. The border proceeds overland.* ⁸*The border becomes The Río Bonito. We are beautiful. A river. It goes south. We went south.* ⁹*The border reaches the Pedernales River. You and me. We.* ¹⁰*The border and the river touch the sea.*

-as in-

21. The border:

-as in-

Along the border
On a dirt road
On a drive to el campo
You found a batey
I cut the cane
We sucked on a stalk
You gave me your arms
I swam in the river
We locked the door
the lights went out
the radio played
You fingered the pesos
I walked to the beach
We fried the fish
You ate the mango
I jumped in the water
We bought the flowers
Then the migrants came
And you bartered for more
Then the sirens blared
And they were carried away
But we didn't stop them
Then the ocean swept
And the palm trees sagged
They were foreigners
We were foreigners
And this was home

<u>**Act I**</u>

Act I Set Design- Map

Directions:

Look at the description below[8]
Use the space provided
to map
the set design
for Act I-
before the cutting

[8]*Avocado bellied hills. On hills. On hills. The forest folds in on itself. Fertile fields. Ripe crops. Cane ready for harvest. A river runs through it.*

<u>Act I</u>

<u>Scene 1</u>

Setting: Chalk white clouds. A bed of copper
         soil. Crimson dawn. A border of fish
         and flesh crossing.

At Rise: An empty altar. The sound of water.

MADAME TELSAINT

We run

IRELIA

like bodies seeking rest
staccattoed, borderless notes
from a trumpet stuttering bap bap bap

MADAME TELSAINT

We pray

CENALIA

hands in search of light
clothes washed in the river
lame legs and crippled tongues
across a friendship bridge

MADAME TELSAINT

We sing

CAMERON

parroted syllables swallowed
for survival

MADAME TELSAINT

We sleep

CENALIA

in liquid fields cut and burned for harvest
coconut milk, silk and soil
a horizon of flame trees burning the sky red

MADAME TELSAINT

We are

IRELIA

larimar waves spilling
seafoam salt onto sand

CENALIA

buried bones lifted
out of unmarked graves

CAMERON

a wind, a city of ash

MADAME TELSAINT

We rise and dance on air

Scene 2

(The hills become a hospital. The
river becomes a bed. The border
becomes a wall.)

ME

The wounds had been made by a machete.
But America didn't care about us as a news story.
And in a hospital along the border,
     men, women, and children lay severed
Limb stumps pulsing angry red against black skin.

And while America didn't care about us as a news story,
Irelia Gideon (9), Cenalia Pierre (22), Cameron Pean (11)
Lay severed limb stumps pulsing angry,
     red against black skin.
Whole families fleshed by the flashing fury of a machete.

Survivors like Irelia, Cenalia, and Cameron
Cried out, clenched fists, trilled tongues
     and swallowed screams,
Whole families fleshed red—a fury of flashing machetes,
Asking: What had they done to deserve this?

Crying out, clenched fist, tongue trills
     and swallowed screams,
Thousands of butchered bodies buried
     beneath ravines burn
With, why? What had they done to deserve this—
Separated (s)kin and bone felled from flesh,
     floating down a river

Red with thousands of butchered bodies
     bobbing and burning along ravines.

There was only one who denied it—
the president of Santo Domingo
Separated (s)kin, felled bone from flesh
        and sent it floating down a river

Red, while Irelia, Cenalia, and Cameron remember
The only one who denied it—
the president of Santo Domingo.
In a hospital along the border, men, women, and children
like Irelia, Cenalia, and Cameron, remember
Their wounds, made by a machete.

        (Blackout)

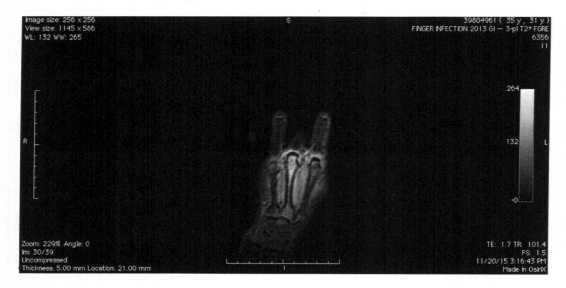

Papi says we are what we do. With our hands. At age nine I curl my fingers around the shell of a coconut. He shows me how to use a machete. The blade turns and winks at me. We catch the sunlight. I wince, my hands afraid of the cut. Of the blood that could tremble or trickle down a knuckle. Papi says the machete is built for reaping and revolution, farming, and food. Papi names his machete. A tool. Like the hammer or the pen. He wraps his fingers around mine. We grip the machete. We raise it above our heads. Papi says do not be afraid of the machete. But I do not want to carry the weight of a weapon in my hands.

MACHETE

call me what you want

gift / weapon / thief

from the inside out a CT scan
slices you a photograph
you cannot forget a memory
you cannot hold

Dominican - American / Haitian -
American / American - American

I hyphenate you into the you
that you are tissue rot stem
cells bundle of knuckles
harvest of fingertips

hold still / just breathe / count to ten

I swing

after the fog a rusty tongue
sticks and clicks your heavy metal
breath a metronome marks
my song a ballad that begins
and ends in blood

a cacophony of green hands and blue
mouths migrate towards your borders
draw a line where they will pull
apart your ligaments to collect
scars cut from the altar
of your almost fist

steel cut / sharp needle / silk scalpel

your stemmed finger a rot root
eviction notice where blood trembles
and I belong bent like stripped winds

soft / silent / serene

sink under then sleep between
saltgrass and palmas

I swing

call me by my name

Kukiri / Hawkbill / Cane

        (Blackout)

INTERLUDE

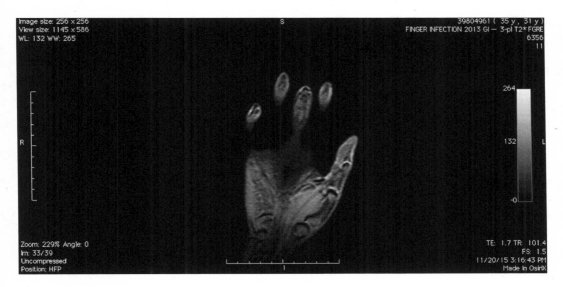

The name they give it is Scleroderma from the Latin meaning hard-skin. It thickens. Thick-skin is supposed to protect. Instead I harden and hurt all over. Tiny ulcers form and fester on the tips of my fingers. Cuticles blister, burn and erupt, a volcano of pus and blood the skin, the nail, the bone a slow decay of rotting cells that refuse to heal. There is nothing left to do but amputate. My wounds will be made by a scalpel. Not a machete. But I too will be cut. Pieces of me will also go missing. Where will they end up? When a foreign substance invades the body, the body attacks it. To try to heal itself. If that doesn't work then you cut into the skin and drag the foreign substance out. But what happens when the body attacks itself? How do you heal when you are the weapon and the wound?

Scene 4

(Rice. Pots. Water. River rushing.
Swish. Swish. Swish. The women
pour. An offering.)

MADAME TELSAINT

If I can't return to water,
then lay me on a bed of rice.

ME

I shake blue river stones, and white
pebbles in my palm. I shake rice
in a bowl to hear a rain song.

CENALIA

I let my fingers settle in
the bowl, a history of hunger,
a harvest too little to count.

IRELIA

I turn the grains round,
round my knuckles.

MADAME TELSAINT

A fistful
of what makes the heart go
soft. They chalk my skin
white. A saint. A cleansing.
A dusting of remains.

CENALIA

I roll these farm pearls
between my fingers--

IRELIA

diamonds on dark skin--

                    ME
a starry night en el campo.

             MADAME TELSAINT
Add water to the bowl slow
and across, the way you might
bless yourself in cathedral.

                  CENALIA
A rush of wet pebbles skins
the surface.

             MADAME TELSAINT
Rinse and wash.
Rinse and wash.

                  IRELIA
Baby teeth
of the soil.

             MADAME TELSAINT
Thread the obsidian ones--the dirty,
rice--out. They are not fit
for baptism.

                  CENALIA
They are crushed seashells
plucked from a bed
of sand.

                  IRELIA
We cook rice because it grows a small fist-
full can feed a family of five or ten.

             MADAME TELSAINT
Drain the mulch into your
palm and feel how it weighs

with water and clings to skin--

                    CENALIA
a second offering.

                    MADAME TELSAINT
Rice gives without asking
for anything in return

                    IRELIA
it satisfies a need
to be satisfied.

                    MADAME TELSAINT
Spoon the blessed
crystals out and toss them
into the silver pot.

                    ME
The saltwater whispers

                    CENALIA
steam--a love
song to my lashes.

                    IRELIA
Listen as the pot hums.

                    ME
I look for what may remain
of my mother's mother
and her mother's mother and all
the mothers we will never know.

                    MADAME TELSAINT
We watch as the grains of rice grow.

(Sunrise. Green. Rolling hills.
River rushing. A chair. Rocks.
Back. Forth. Back. Forth.)

ME

Madame T, what is Haiti like?

MADAME TELSAINT

Why do you want to know?

ME

Because I've never been on the other side
of the island.

MADAME TELSAINT

What do you want to know?

ME

Do your trees birth bundles
of plátanos every full moon
and do the women breastfeed
three or four babies in one
year?

MADAME TELSAINT

No. Your stories are *maji*, my dear.

ME

Then tell me the color of the mountains
across the river and how the wind breathes.

MADAME TELSAINT

Gen, sanble yon anpil tankou isit la.
Gen santi l anpil tankou isit la.
The drums, the wind, the way the river inhales,
and the palm trees sigh, it's all the same. Except
our syllables sing and our voices shake

the earth open to swallow us up
every hundred years.

(Sugar cane. Smoke. Rustling
leaves. Storm winds.)

MADAME TELSAINT

Once, I ran away
with my beloved who wrapped me
in plantain leaves and sugar soil
his honey hands dripped
along my thighs
his molasses mouth circled
my tulip breasts and my body
filled with wildfire
a cane field harvested
with fertile flames

He resurrected the woman in me
and I emerged summoning spirits
from el mas allá
Ay
        Ay
                Ay

Amaryllis sage smoke
frankincense and myrrh
a Palo drum dance beating between us
my back a bridge
his tongue knew how to cross
my hair a midnight forest
his hands were not afraid to find
my sex pink petals he tongued
and stroked until we were wet
with sweat and morning mist

My breath blew out the light
of a candle beneath a billowing
bannann tree he rested
his lips on the altar
of my hips and I became his
negra

       (Blackout)

INTERLUDE

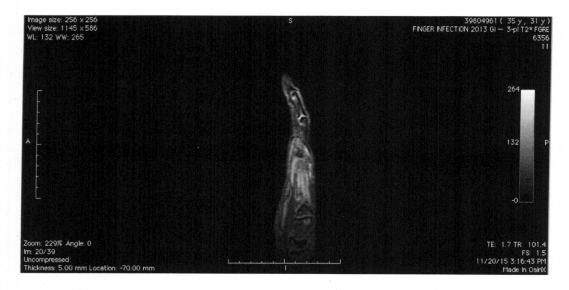

Negro. Black. Purple. Blue. White. Green. Black. But never red. Never red again. My finger failed to flow with blood, so it turned black instead. The name they give this is ischemia from the Greek meaning stopping blood. What started as a hangnail became a hole in the earth of my fingertips and bone. I scratched the tomato paste wound where blood once crusted on the nail but it sloshed a muddy brown waxed black and lost all its warmth. I yelled into this ivory green well, scraped black dahlias from its walls, unearthed a field of star dust and decay. I asked the doctor to save it. Not enough oxygen in the blood for it to breathe. My finger--river bent, looked the other way, a part of me always searching for who/what we've left behind.

Scene 5

(White flowers. Honey.
Coins. An offering. A fertility
ritual. The ocean.)

CENALIA

Root, glide ground my soles
in the sand stand royal
and carry heavy loads
on my head a crown
of guavas mangos yucca
corn beans molasses
and white dahlias
in white baskets

Seven fistfuls of silver
a bundle of palms
and petals a slick tongue
skims the water slides
into a muddy throat
that asks for more
                        more

                                        more

Like hands buried
in hair I sink
into the ocean
open my womb a leaf
scarred queen palm tree
and wait for it to carry
a memory of light

47

(The sun. Flame trees fluttering.
A river rushing.)

IRELIA

Manman
says I'm not supposed to run
by the river
but *Manman* doesn't know how
good it feels. Like mermaid kisses
from the sea, I love the way the wet
grass tickles my toes when I skip
and splash the women washing
clothes and hair.

Manman
says not to run on the river
rocks when the sun hangs
over the water like a ripe mango
ready to drop. Because that's when the soil
burns the skin and my feet
she says, will blister red hot
into a flame tree.

Manman
says I shouldn't run with the boys
down the river bank
because girls who want to
marry should always walk.
But I'm the fastest runner
in Dajabón. Faster than Gustav
and Eugene and Vincent. Faster
because they'll pull
the white ribbons in my hair
if they catch me. Faster
because I eat less and never look back.

(Sugar cane. Green. Soil. Wind.
The ocean.)

MADAME TELSAINT

My beloved's back
is bent from breaking
stalks before they would rot
His fingers swelled with soil
his palms scrubbed black
I'd lick the sugar
from beneath his nails
he'd whisper
"Ay mi negra,
    negra mia,
        ay mi negra."

       "Negra sucia!"

Papa yelled when he finally found
us covered in starshine and red
clay cackling in the cane fields he pulled
a machete from his sling swung
it across his body split
my beloved and made him sing

He sank and cupped my face
I slipped into his hands
clung to his touch skinned
my lashes beneath his heart
his chin the shadow of my hair
he surrendered my skin
my heart a soil of want

(Green. Blades of grass. Snakes
hiss. An echo. Another voice. In
the distance. An offering.)

CAMERON

Learn to kill
animals

          chase their tails
          snap their necks

with fists
and hunger

Learn to swim
in the river

          swim and gather
          the current

arms and mud
between your toes

Learn to cut
fruit from a tree

          with your teeth
          rip the skin off

mangoes, a memory
that bleeds

Learn to follow
the light

          the moon
          trap starshine

inside your palms
trap farolitos   in the dark

Try to make it
home with food
in your pockets

50

                        search
                        for almonds
picked from blades
of grass
                        for brothers
                        you didn't get
to bury

            (Blackout)

INTERLUDE

We call it a Rosary. I bury my hands in sand and pray. You do not need beads to pray. Ten fingers. Ten prayers or just one finger sliced ten times. Our father who art in heaven, like my father's side of the family whose last name was and is del Rosario. Hail Mary, Nuestra Señora del Rosario patron saint of the city of Dajabón, pray for those who died on your feast day. Holy Mary mother of God, my mother prays the rosary over each one of my fingers every night before she goes to bed because there is no burial, ceremony, funeral, memorial or marker for a body part ripped from its root and sent down a river. Instead we name it limb and loss.

<u>Act II</u>

Act II Set Design- Map

Directions:

Look at the description below[9]
Use the space provided
to map
the set design
for Act II-
the cutting

---

[9]*Green moon like a green coin. Harvested cane burns. Gauze of skinny gray smoke. The river runs red.*

INTERLUDE

Ciudad Trujillo, Santo Domingo, DR
October 11, 1937.
Subject: Slaughter of Haitians on Northwest
Frontier.
The Honorable
The Secretary of State,
Washington DC

Sir:
I have the honor to confirm my telegram No.
30 of October 11- 9am., reporting that
approximately one thousand Haitian residents
on the northwest frontier of the Dominican
Republic had been killed by the Dominican
national Police and Army…a systemic campaign
of extermination was directed against all
Haitian residents…As a result of this
campaign, the entire northwest frontier on
the Dajabón side is absolutely devoid of
Haitians. Those not slain either fled across
the frontier or are still hiding in the bush.

Telegram sent from
US Ambassador to the Dominican Republic, R.
Henry Norweb to to Secretary of State Cordell
Hull, 11/10/1937

Dominicans and Haitians campaign for one frontier-As a result, the police & army slaughter Haitians in the bush. Report the slain, hide the slaughter, flee the bush! Dominicans direct Haitians across this side of the frontier-As a result, police slaughter Dominicans hiding Haitians in the bush. Flee the campaign, report the slaughter, army the bush! Honor the slain, flee the slaughter, hide the bush! Bushed Haitians report the slaughter on the northwest frontier-As a result, the police hide the report and flee the bush. Police the report, kill the campaign, slaughter the bush! Slaughter the army, kill the police, honor the bush.

Act II

Scene 1

Setting: Whipped ash blankets the sky. Palm trees
swat at the dim breeze. A cane field.

At Rise: The altar is complete. The sky coughs.
Smoke-filled air. Smells of parsley.

MACHETE

First there was nothing \ then there was wound
a closed fist slippery with sweat \ wrinkled with work--
I live in that starless place between fingers \ wrist

A farmer wakes to collect his crop \ I clip
the stem of a plátano \ press its skin against
my cheek \ salt my gums with its meat

A parched young choirboy wants a drink of summer
sunshine, so I strike swollen coconut skulls wet
with milk \ take a sip with him

A lover carves his bride-to-be a chair to rock
her unborn children in \ I spoon splintered wood \ lap
the brown bark with my hungry mouth

I thrust my tongue against cane \ cut my teeth
on its peel fine nectar for migrants who want to
feed their families \ their longing
something sweeter than sugar

The soldier \ the surgeon tries to imitate the hand
of God, raise \ render me silent when I split

stubborn bone in half \ cannot shake the bitters
of blood that clot my shine

I would never take what isn't mine

Scene 2

(A loud crack. Storm winds.
Cackling leaves. The altar sways.
MACHETE becomes SOLDIER.)

SOLDIER

Where were you born?

CAMERON

Here.

SOLDIER

¿Donde usted nació?

IRELIA

Aquí.

SOLDIER

Where were you born?

MADAME TELSAINT

Here.

SOLDIER

¿Donde usted nació?

CENALIA

Aquí.

SOLDIER

Where were you born?

ME

Here/ Aquí.

(Green. Flicker of light.
Boot stomps. The altar shakes.)

SOLDIER

The air feathered green rotted like mold
Fireflies danced and lit up the night
I'd drink aguardiente real fast not slow
Burn out the guilt and blurry my sight
Swallow smoke and a prayer for my very own soul
First we cleared the earth and dug the holes
Then we cut the ears and drained the wax
Stuffed matches between their sullied toes
Waited for skin and bone, to pop and crack
Then we set it all ablaze con fósforos

(Red. Fire. Smoke. The
river. Whispers. Become
screams. The altar. Trembles.)

IRELIA

pe_rejil   perejil   perejil   tijera colorada

CENALIA

pe_rejil   pe_rejil   perejil   tije a colo ada

CAMERON

pe ejil perejil pe ejil   tijera colorada   perejil   pe ejil

CENALIA

tije^ra colo_rada   perejil   tije a colo ada   perejil

IRELIA

perejil pe_rejil tijera colorada   perejil   pe_rejil

CAMERON

tijera colo_rada pe ejil   peRejil   tijeRa colo^Rada

MADAME TELSAINT

(Blackout)

INTERLUDE

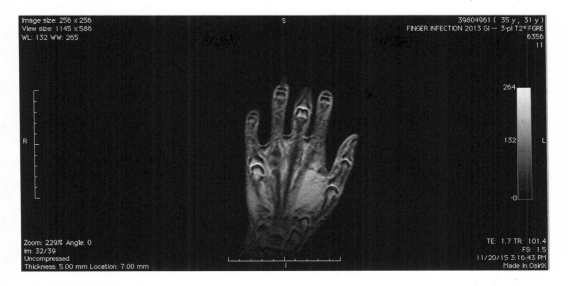

Una tijera colorada, a red scissor was used to cut the bandage off my surgically severed fingertip. The nurse unraveled the gauze. One single cross-stitch scar stretched across the bone. There would be no more wash, rinse, wrap, and repeat. There would be no more infection or gangrene. There would be no more fingertip, fingerprint, or nail. Just this--a phantom pain pulsing--the final remedy.

Scene 3

(Rustling leaves. Wind.)

CAMERON

Gloria! Rips and scars inside my body
Roll it like perejil, perejil
like limoncillo between my lips
Pink and ready to fill with song

Gloria, I roll it like perejil, perejil
Don't let the r lie flat, weak
and pink--ready it with song
and ribs a trembling cage inside my throat

       (Soldier. Sniff. Lift. Machete. Listen
       for the squeal. Shibboleth. An ear. Pressed.
       To the ground.)

an (ea)r lies weak and flat
Follow the trill, lift the tongue
a caged tremble, a rib inside the throat,
almost silent, almost music

Follow the trill, lift the tongue
like limoncillo between the lips
almost silent, almost music--sing
Perejil, perejil, a ripped scar inside the body

(The river rushing.)

IRELIA

Manman
said run that night. But I couldn't
lift my legs. *Manman* pushed
me into the rain. It hit my eyes
and I couldn't see *Manman*
also afraid of running from the men
coming to get us. And my feet sank
into the mud because I thought
the earth could save us. I felt her
hand pull mine. And we ran
towards the dark of the river
the dark of the night
but even the dark couldn't
hide us.

Manman
said run, Irelia, run
when a full moon man raised
a machete and dropped it
cutting *Manman*'s arm
away from mine. Another tried
to break my head open
like a coconut, it cracked
and *Manman* screamed her words
drowned in the river current:
"Run, Irelia, run!"

> (Soldier lunges. Irelia ducks. Soldier
> slices. Irelia slips. Through his fingers.
> Irelia runs.)

Manman
said run so I ran and I didn't

look back. *Manman* said run
and I ran so they wouldn't
catch me and pull
the white ribbons in my hair.
Manman said run and I ran fast
because the others were running
and I ran faster. Faster
than Gustav and Eugene and Vincent
because they didn't know.
And I ran with blood
in my eyes and I ran with fear
in my feet and I ran without
looking back and I ran without
Manman.

(A baby cries.)

CENALIA

Tethered to my breast he is anchor in an ocean of milk.
Pull and suck. Surge and swim inside the black milk

of his pupils. I sway, a hammock where we both can look
into each other's sky. Latch on, let down, milk

out liquid light. His pink lips wrap around the hibiscus
buds of my breast, a hummingbird suckling sap, milk

shifts, shooting stars granting wishes in his hungry mouth.
Buzz, breathe, flicker, flutter, a rush of warmth, milk

my skin, his skin, my body, his body, he drinks and drinks,
opens and closes his eyes, my milk, his milk

       (Soldier. Machete. Baby. Bent. Baby. Up in
       the air. Falls. Machete. Slash. Gather. Hold.
       Baby. Bosom. Milk.)

splashes and bruises the wet red ground. My son!
my son, crushed like baby's breath in a bowl without milk.

Hallelujah! Hallelujah! I suck and pull my curdled breast
Hallelujah, Hallelujah sinks and drowns in rivers of milk.

(Soldier. Circles Madame Telsaint. She holds.
Her head up. Soldier pushes her. Down. She
falls. He pulls. Her hair. Soldier. Machete.
A single scream.)

MADAME TELSAINT

(The altar. Has fallen.)

(Blackout)

INTERLUDE

For **SEVEN** days and **SEVEN** nights, soldiers chopped, and cut human flesh and bone until Trujillo was satisfied. Afterwards, they were said to have gone mad. Mumbling in the night. Sobbing in their sleep. Regret crawling like spiders beneath their skin.

For **SIX** months we cleaned my wounds and waited for my
finger to heal. Hand surgeon. Rheumatologist. Wound care
specialist. Physical therapist. "Therapist" therapist.
Antibiotics. Vicodin. Tramadol. Sleep. My chronic pain
was becoming a cliché.

Dominicans received a **TWENTY-FOUR** hour notice to leave Dajabón before the soldiers came.

I received **TWENTY-FOUR** days of hyperbaric chamber oxygen treatments because someone told me it had worked for them and saved their foot.

More than **TWO THOUSAND** ethnic Haitians were able to escape along the border on foot. How many more could have been saved if only they had known?

The Dominican government paid **$525,000** in reparations to Haitian survivors. Of the **$30** allotted to each survivor, each survivor was paid only **2** cents each. They were fortunate. They survived.

Survival is a luxury afforded only to the fortunate. I paid more than **SEVEN THOUSAND** dollars to repair what was already damaged. $7000 in 2021 is equivalent to $132,983.96 in 1937. This is 40% of what was paid to survivors. I could afford it. *I am fortunate.*

A weighted estimate of **464,026** patients sustained finger amputations in the US from 1997 to 2016.

An estimate of **12,000? 15,000? 20,000?** Haitians and/or Dominicans were killed or suffered amputations during the massacre. There is no accurate account of how much was lost.

Scene 4

(Fire. Darkness. They dance. Around
the altar.)

MADAME TELSAINT

We are
     the salt
          the earth

CENALIA

     thrown out hit
the ground-

IRELIA

     thud, a steel-toed boot
on wooden planks

CAMERON

     scatter and roll
          lodge between
floorboards and bark,

CENALIA

          hide until it is safe
               to return-

IRELIA

or never be seen again

MADAME TELSAINT

Can the earth survive
     without its salt?

CENALIA

          When you don't know
               it's coming

                    CAMERON
          an ocean wave will slap
               salt in your eye

                    IRELIA
     pulse up your nostrils

                    CENALIA
     sashay around
          your tongue

                    CAMERON
          ripple into the back
               of your throat

               MADAME TELSAINT
          crust on the sides
     of your mouth

                    IRELIA
          dry out
               your words

                    CENALIA
     Salt is not
          easily forgotten

                    CAMERON
     The body was never meant to be
               silent

                    ME
          There are things the eyes
               were never meant to see

                    CENALIA
          Leave the salt

                in the earth

                          IRELIA
        Leave the salt
              in the water

                     MADAME TELSAINT
        Leave the salt   alone

            (Blackout)

INTERLUDE

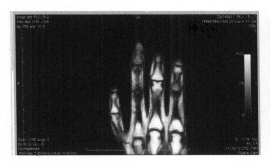 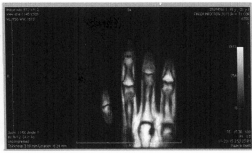

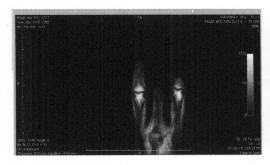 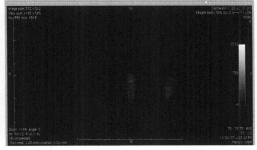

Before the cutting I tested positive. On a pregnancy test. I was asked if I still wanted anesthesia. Given the risks. I said no. I should have been given anesthesia. I remember the blue sheet. You wade in the river with everyone in it. Collect stones and clay. Build a body that cannot be. Broken. I remember the glare. Of the scalpel. You take the machete. Turn the blade the other way. I remember green scrubs. You climb hills and drag sugarcane. To reach the other side. Time and touch slips through my fingers. My knuckle knocks on a metal plate. Your wrist sinks into the dirt. False positive pregnancy test. My womb was empty. I should have been given anesthesia. You never should have been cut. We drown in limbs and in losses we cannot count.

Scene 5

(White light. White cloth. Wind.
The ocean.)

MADAME TELSAINT

Everything begins and ends with a name
spirits, saints, phantom limbs and phantom
pains the machete is not to blame but the hand
that wields him again and again

Split caña rums the earth a sugarcane
grave splintered skin soaks the soil red
river bubbling with what we could not save

My hands sweat and bless harvest flames
rooted beneath the soil souls scratch
and toil itch and listen for someone
to shake or willow whisper their names

CAMERON PEAN

!Presente!

IRELIA GIDEON

!Presente!

CENALIA PIERRE

!Presente!

MADAME TELSAINT

!Presente!

(Write the names. Of the ones you have lost. In the blanks provided. If you run out of blanks use the margins. If you run out of margins use your palms. If you run out of palms use your tongue. Lift their names up until someone else can hear it.)

———————————

!Presente!

———————————

!Presente!

———————————

!Presente!

———————————

!Presente!

———————————

!Presente!

!Presente!   _____

!Presente!   _____

!Presente!   _____

!Presente!   _____

!Presente!   _____

!Presente!   _____

!Presente!   _____

!Presente!   _____

!Presente!   _____

!Presente!   _____

Scene 6

(Darkness. Deep blue. Or gangrene.
Mud prints. On the floor. A hiss. A
single beam. Of light. Cuts the
air. The flicker. Of a flame.
Remembering.)

MACHETE

I drag your name out of the swamp
heavy with honey and mud it is not
an easy root to pull

/ / /

I slip into the tree carve
name between slivers of chipped bark
early sunlight let its sap syrup
hum hymn and break the shine
behind my blade

/ / /

Your name is a cicada for years
it turns the soil inside a throat
that shuts like a border when I lean in
too close to kiss it hoping the vowels
and consonants will scurry out
hissing and shrilling for light

/ / /

I crawl your name into the cane
fields lift and lunge it between blades
of morning dew shred its echo
into winged syllables I won't forget

/ / /

I make your name a feather
so the wind will want to carry you
with it

/ / /

Your name is a map I drop
and unfurl on the kitchen table. I follow
its foothills and valleys with the tip
of my blade trace its lines and letters in
dust and sand spell only *river*

/ / /

I stroke the fingers of your name watch it
roll away like a weary *rr* or a severed head
of lettuce. Rub my quiet along its cheek and feel
almost nothing when it turns to look
the other way

/ / /

I yearn to put your name back
inside a mouth like a last breath
or a lost tooth only a mother would keep

Scene 7

(Sunlight. The River. They rebuild
the altar.)

MADAME TELSAINT

We are

ME

a cadence beating beneath the soil

MADAME TELSAINT

We are

CAMERON

the voice of the River Massacre

MADAME TELSAINT

We are

IRELIA

emptied homes haunting
the island left to right

MADAME TELSAINT

We are

CENALIA

a crescendo of Creole

MADAME TELSAINT

We are

ME

a streamcut gorge flooded with sound

MADAME TELSAINT
We are

IRELIA
a symphony of souls
a forgotten measure

ME
a shoreline shadow of washed up rags & feet

CAMERON
a deep valley ravine humming in the hillside

CENALIA
We are a Dajabón sky concerto

CAMERON
We are a Caribbean verse

ME
We are a hurricane of hands

IRELIA
We are a refugee lyric

CAMERON
We are a requiem

MADAME TELSAINT
We are the ocean

We are its memory

We are ssssh sssshh ssshh

(Lights Up)

FINAL INTERLUDE

A new ulcer has begun to form on the fourth digit of my right hand and it's **refusing to heal.** I'm not as eager to start cutting this time. A new ulcer has begun to form on the fourth digit of **my right hand** and it's **refusing to heal.** I'm not as eager to start cutting this time. A new ulcer has begun to form on the fourth digit of **my right hand** and it's refusing to heal. I'm not as **eager** to start cutting this time. **A new ulcer** has begun to form on the fourth digit of my right hand and it's **refusing to heal.** I'm not as eager to **start cutting** this time.

END OF PLAY

PRODUCTION NOTES

I.   A NOTE ABOUT CASTING: See "INHERITANCE" and do the opposite.

II. A NOTE ABOUT INTERLUDES: Projections on a screen. The present. Meets the past. A look. Inside. Do not look. The other way. There is always. More. To see.

III. A NOTE ABOUT MOVEMENT: A hurricane of hands. Hands in search of light. Hands. Beating beneath the soil. Hands. That move. Hands that dance. On air.

IV. A NOTE ABOUT LIGHTING: The color green should fester. An echo we can smell. Blue should slip. Like water between our fingers. Red will burn. Lightening between our knees. The light. Should make us see things. That are not there. Blackouts should reveal. What we are too afraid. To admit. What the throat cannot bear. To say.

V.   A NOTE ABOUT SOUND: The trees. The hills. The soil. The river. The ocean. The cane. The sky. Are louder than the voices on the stage/page. Are there even when the voices are not.

VI. PROPS LIST: See "HOW TO BUILD AN ALTAR"

HOW TO BUILD AN ALTAR

Gather photos--

scribble the names of the dead
on the back of your hands
name each finger until you run out
of hands or names or fingers
fold them into flowers and plant them
in the pages of this book
water them with want and waiting
kneel until they night-blossom
into palms or prayers
we will one day hold and inherit

Make an offering--

a bounty	of rice
a twirl	of white ribbons
a shot	of rum
a slip	of sand
a bed	of water
a bouquet	of hair
a scent	of lilies
a mural	of elegies
almonds	chocolate
sugarcane	silver coins
blue stones	red clay
a bib	a whisper
un cigarro	un suspiro
y una muñeca	sin rostro

Ask questions--

What is the body without a name?

                              Where am I from?

Are you sure we're not Haitian?

                              Where have we been

Where is home   without a border?

                              Where are you from?

Could we be Haitian?

                              Why do you want to know?

Pray--

You are here

                                                    I am here

                    We are here

          We are still here

Say Their Names--

95

III

The Myth

You began in a sterile room. Where I prayed. To whatever lives in heaven that the fire in me would not burn you. Out. The way it had another seed that slipped into the soil at my feet. A blue-eyed man used his gloved hands to transfer your constellation. Set with stars into the river of my uterus. You began to swim in my connective tissue. A pin prick of light. You burrowed in the banks of my abdomen. Made a home in my lower back. The weight of my wait for you wrapped around my waist. Grew heavier every week. I was a house trying to house the sun. You were a myth. Until I knew the sound of your heartbeat. Like I know now the sound of your voice. One always louder than the other.

The Forgotten

The highway is littered with stuff. Stuff people no longer want. Big stuff. Old stuff. Broken stuff. A white cooler's blue lid flaps in the wind. A once upon a good time. A brown leather recliner wobbles and waits by the side of the road. A hitchhiker waiting for a home. A full size mattress springs and wails. A purple velvet ottoman puts on a show and sullies in the rain. A used up memory no one will claim. At night, while I wait for you to wake. While I wait to fall asleep. I close my eyes and count the stuff I've seen. Sheep in a field of almost dreams. Cantankerous treasures tossed to the side. One. Two. Three. Mami would say: "Que lastima. Such good things. Gone to waste." I imagine a highway of almost apologies. Words between Mami and I that got used up. Thrown on the curb. Forgotten. "Que lastima," I whisper into the dark. There is an almost whimper in the monitor. It bends into prayer. It leaks into the cracks between us. Mothers. Daughters. Begins to fix what we don't want. To throw away.

The Mother

She sits in a bathtub. Knees pressed against her chest. Head tucked between her thighs. Water falls from a shower head and drowns out everyone else's cries. Questions. Demands. Desires. It's the only time of day she has to herself. She'll take whatever she can get. Five. Ten. Fifteen. Twenty. Minutes alone. She can think in here. If she wants to. Or not. She can cry. Or sob. Hear the sound of her own breath. Her own voice. Her own skin. She'll scrub with soap the remnants of dried food. Dried milk. Dried snot. She won't even remember who it all belongs to. She'll study the length of her nails. Her leg hairs. Her arms. And how much they have to carry. To reach for. She'll rub her back. Hips. Thighs. Breasts. Remember when they belonged only to her.

The Father

He wants to kiss my neck. Cup my breasts. Hold my thighs between his hands. I tell him: No. Not today. Not right now. I turn away. When he holds me. Cringe. When his breath gets too close. He wants to know: What's wrong? Why I prefer bed sheets against my hips. To the rub of his fingertips. Why I smile at the rain on my face. But not at the dew of his lips on my cheeks.

All day you, my baby girl, claw at my neck. My face. My cheeks. My thighs. My breasts. Your rice patty hands press and palm into me. I am dough. You are a bread maker. Your runny nose gnaws at my ear and blesses me. Your mouth gums my face. It tickles. You eat my chin. You take a fist full of my hair in your hands. You devour me. I am yours.

My body has become soft fruit. Plum breasts. Overripe honeydew butt. Browned apple belly. Peeled banana arms left out on the counter too long. So much of me sags.

At night, Iholdmybodyclose, when he tries to u n r a v e l it.

The Fable

Smile. If only because you recognize my face in the face of other women. Remember what we have escaped. What we have done to each other. The light-skinned women. To the dark-skinned women. How you are one. And I am the other. How I am one. And someone else is the other. Remember this Mestizaje-African Fable: A green river slides into an ocean of bones. A sea of rot. So much to recover. But it's not anything anyone else would want. Somewhere beneath, our skin to skin is making its way into my DNA. Changing how I carry the women who made it. Out of the water.

The Silver Spoon

I pull out of your mouth. Fumbles out of my right hand. Again. I cannot clutch my fingers around it. It is small. I feel small. You open your small mouth. Your sticky. Wet. Pink tongue. Reaches out. Dragon fruit tentacles explode in my direction. Your chin juts forward. You are a baby. Bird. Waiting for worms. Your palms open. Close. Open. Close. This is your sign for *more. ¿Más? ¿Más?* Your head bobbles left. Right. Up. Down. Yes. No.

I set the spoon inside the bowl. Fold my hands into shadow puppets. A left and right mouth opens. Closes. I try to teach you. Baby sign language. My left hand becomes a less than symbol. My right hand becomes greater than. I tap my fingertips together. *Más. Más.* I use three fingers. Instead of five. Because my scleroderma has left me. With less than. A middle fingertip. With less than. Straight knuckles. With less than. Limited mobility. How do you use your hands. To ask for *more*. When you do not have. Enough.

I scoop up the silver spoon. With all the fingers of my right hand. My pincer grip is not as precise as yours. Anymore. I trace a letter C in your bowl. Fill the spoon up. With just enough to feed you. My skin pulls. Tightens. A pulsing throb. Beneath the nail. A small tremor. A tiny earthquake. Inside my wrist. My knuckle buckles. Under the weight of the spoon. The food tumbles. Falls. Again.

Your soft baked potato fingers reach for the clump. Green mush. I have spilled. Your palms smash it down. You giggle. You are learning to understand the world. By how it feels. In your hands. Sometimes the world slips through. Your fingers. Sometimes you can hold it firm. Throw it. Bang it together. Put it in your mouth. Sometimes you want to carry more than your hands can hold.

I wipe the food away. I am used to making messes. You reach for the silver spoon. I let you. Hold it. I let you feel what it feels like. In your unsteady hands. You lift it up to your nose. Nope. That's not right. You lift it up to your eyes. Still too high. You lower it down to your chin. You've made a mess. All over. Your face. I do not wipe it away. We laugh.

With my good hand, I pull the moon out of your tight fist. I promise to feed you. The stars.

The Final Blackout
May 30

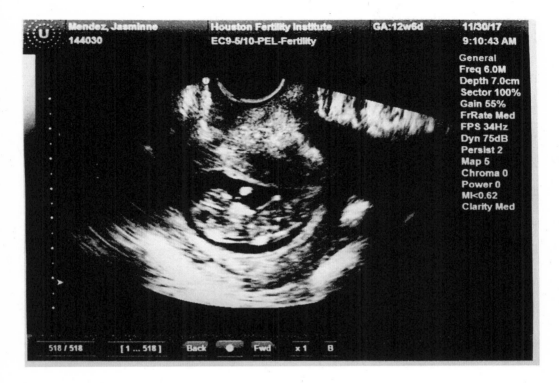

You are a lullaby that trembles on the tongue and kicks at the teeth. You are the Z inside your name. You were meant to vibrate down the body. You are the frozen embryo baby. Constellations and moon. The cluster of cells I held inside my womb. Poppy seed. Apricot. Papaya. Honey-dew. Grow and grow. Then: contract and sweat. Push and show: arms, legs, heart and head. Unspool away from my ribs. Breathe. Burp. Blink. Smoke black hair. Howling lungs. Dimpled neck. Ten fingers. Ten toes. Tight grip around my missing fingertip. I am not whole. But I am enough. Somos lucha. Eres mía. Your hand in my hand––the light that slips in even after the final curtain has closed.

The Names[10]

------------------   ------------------   ------------------

------------------   ------------------   ------------------

------------------   ------------------   ------------------

------------------   ------------------   ------------------

------------------   ------------------   ------------------

------------------   ------------------   ------------------

------------------   ------------------   ------------------

------------------   ------------------   ------------------

------------------   ------------------   ------------------

------------------   ------------------   ------------------

------------------   ------------------   ------------------

------------------   ------------------   ------------------

------------------   ------------------   ------------------

------------------   ------------------   ------------------

------------------   ------------------   ------------------

[10]*Please write the names of the ones you **have** in the blanks provided. If you run out of blanks use the margins. If you run out of margins use your palms. If you run out of palms use your tongue and lift their names up until someone else can hear it.*

NOTES

"Inheritance" is indebted to Tarfia Faizullha's book of poems Seam, Southern Illinois University Press, 2014.

"All Roads Lead to" uses found text from a Wikipedia description of where the border runs between the Dominican Republic and Haiti.

"Along the Border" is after Idra Novey's poem "Nearly."

All of the names used in "Characters" and found in the section "City Without Altar" were names of actual victims and survivors of the massacre found in Quentin Reynolds article "Murder in the Tropics", *Collier's*. 22 January 1938.

The persona poems and reimagined dialogue in "City Without Altar" are sourced from and indebted to transcripts from the interviews conducted by Dr. Lauren Derby, Dr. Edward Paulino, and Dr. Richard Lee Turtis with Haitian Massacre survivors, perpetrators, and their families dating back to the 1980s.

"Dramaturgical Notes:"

Notes 1, 16 - The text from these sections can be found on pp 162 of Richard Lee Turtis' book *Foundations of Despotism: Peasants, the Trujillo Regime, and Modernity in Dominican History*. Stanford, CA: Stanford University Press, 2003.

Notes 3, 12 ,15 - Quotes excerpts from Rudolph Mata's *The Surgical Peculiarities of the American Negro*. 1896.

Notes 2, 4, 6, 8, 9, 10, 13, 14, 17 - Facts and information sourced from Richard Lee Turtis' book *Foundations of Despotism: Peasants, the Trujillo Regime, and Modernity in Dominican History*. Stanford, CA: Stanford University Press, 2003 and Lauren Derby's book *The Dictator's Seduction: Politics and the Popular Imagination in the Era of Trujillo*. Durham, NC: Duke University Press, 2009.

Notes 5, 9 - Quotes lines from Rita Dove's poem "Parsley," *Museum*, 1983.

Notes 6, 9, 16 - Definitions sourced from Merriam Webster Online and Wikipedia

Note 7 - Quotes lines from Quentin Reynold's article "Murder in the Tropics", *Collier's.* 22 January 1938.

Note 18 - Quotes lines from Edwidge Danticat's *The Farming of Bones.* New York, NY: Soho Press, Inc., 1998.

"MADAME TELSAINT We rise…" the line *"and dance on air,"* was borrowed from Edwidge Danticat's book *The Farming of Bones.* New York, NY: Soho Press, Inc., 1998.

"ME The wounds had been made…" is a poem compromised of found text from a news article by Quentin Reynolds, "Murder in the Tropics", *Collier's.* 22 January 1938.

Most "Interlude" sections have lines excerpted from the essay "El Corte/The Cutting," originally published in my collection *Night-Blooming Jasmin(n)e: Personal Essays and Poetry.* Arte Público Press, 2018.

"MADAME TELSAINT If I can't return to water…" is indebted to Lena Kahalf Tuffaha's poem "Eating the Earth," from her book *Water & Salt.* Pasadena, CA: Red Hen Press, 2017.

"ME Madame T, what is Haiti like?" was inspired by and is indebted to Lauren Derby's article "Haitians, Magic and Money: Raza and Society in the Haitian-Dominican Borderlands, 1900 to 1937," *Cambridge University Press,* July 1994.

"CENALIA Root, glide…" is after "Knoxville, Tennessee" by Nikki Giovanni.

"IRELIA Manman says I shouldn't…" and "IRELIA Manman said run…" are indebted to Lena Khalaf Tuffaha's poem "Running Orders" from her book *Water & Salt.* Pasadena, CA: Red Hen Press, 2017.

"CAMERON Learn to kill…" Some of the specific details in this poem are indebted to interviews between Dr. Edward Paulino and Haitian Massacre survivors. More information on these interviews can be found in Paulino's book Dividing Hispaniola: *The Dominican Republic's Border Campaign Against Haiti, 1930-1961.* Pittsburgh, PA: University of Pittsburgh Press, 2016.

"SOLDIER Where were you born?" Questions in this section were taken or adapted from interview transcripts between Dr. Lauren Derby and Dr. Richard Lee Turtis and Haitian Massacre survivors. More information on these interviews can be found in Derby's book *The Dictator's Seduction: Politics and the Popular Imagination in the Era of Trujillo*. Durham, NC: Duke University Press, 2009.

"CAMERON Stage Directions..." the lines "An ear. Pressed. To the ground." are indebted to Carolyn Forche's prose poem "The Colonel."

"ME For seven days..." much of this sequence is excerpted from the essay "El Corte/The Cutting," originally published in my collection *Night-Blooming Jasmin(n)e: Personal Essays and Poetry*. Arte Público Press, 2018.

Facts about the Haitian Massacre in this section were excerpted from Richard Lee Turtis' book *Foundations of Despotism: Peasants, the Trujillo Regime, and Modernity in Dominican History*. Stanford, CA: Stanford University Press, 2003 and Edward Paulino's book *Dividing Hispaniola: The Dominican Republic's Border Campaign Against Haiti, 1930-1961*. Pittsburgh, PA: University of Pittsburgh Press, 2016.

"A weighted estimate..." is a statistic found in the article "Epidemiology of Finger Amputations in the United States From 1997 to 2016," *Journal of Hand Surgery Global Online*, Volume 1, Issue 2, April 2019, Pages 45-51.

A note about Interludes: All CT scans are actual scans of my hands and fingers. They were taken in 2015, however the finger I reference had already been amputated in 2013. These are scans from a different finger infection. My doctor's office said scans prior to 2015 had been archived and were no longer available to me. It seems "archives" can become inaccessible.

"The Final Blackout..." is after Juan Felipe Herrera's poem "My Mother's Name Lucha."

ACKNOWLEDGEMENTS

I am grateful to the following journals and anthologies where some of these poems first appeared in various forms

COG Online Magazine
The BreakBeats Poets Volume 4: LatiNEXT
The Long Devotion: Poets Writing Motherhood
The New England Review
Poem-A-Day at Poets.org
Raising Mothers
Split This Rock: The Quarry Poetry Database
The Vassar Review
Zoeglossia: Poem of the Week

This book would not be possible without my ancestors and I must begin by thanking them first. Thank you to Melva "Mamá" Duran, Angel de Jesus "Papito" Duran, Doña Basilia Sosa and Don Juan Tomas Rosario for fighting and for surviving so that I could thrive.

Thank you to my faithful, compassionate and generous editors Carmen Gimenez Smith and J. Michael Martinez who challenged and pushed me and didn't let me give up even when I was ready to hurl this book into the sun. I did not know what my vision was for this book until you shined a light and helped me see it. You pushed me past my comfort zone and both I and this book are better because of it. Thank you also to Sarah Gezmski for her tireless efforts and dedication as we worked through edits and fine tuned every last detail to make this book what it is.

Mil gracias to ALL my writing community and familia. Most especially to Sara Borjas, Vanessa Angélica Villarreal, Addie Tsai, Rosebud Ben-Oni, Gris Muñoz, Icess Fernandez Rojas, Candice D'Meza, Rachel Afi-Quinn and Virginia Grise. You all talked me off a ledge at one point or another during the process of writing this book and made space for me and all of my emotions when I needed it most. Your feedback, words of encouragement and even your care packages were sometimes the only things that allowed me to come back to this work and continue to put words on the page. Thank you hermanas, for reminding me on a daily basis that I matter––that this story matters.

Thank you to my Rainier Writing Workshop family and mentors, Oliver de la Paz, Rick Barot, Rigoberto González, Barrie Jean Borich, Jeric Smith, Kent Weigle, Joanie Strangeland, Libby Hall, Lena Khalaf Tuffaha and all those who saw many of these poems in very early drafts and rooted for me since the start. Thank you also to my Canto Mundo, VONA, Kiskeya Libre and Macondo families for giving me the time, tools and the community I needed to conceive of and eventually write and finish this book. There are too many of you to name, but know that I hold you all near and dear in my heart. Finally, a very special gracias to all of my fellow Dominican writers who have championed this work from the moment I said I wanted to embark on this journey: Yesenia Montilla, Julian Randall, Roberto Carlos Garcia, Dianelly Antigua, Guadalís del Carmen, Peggy Robles Alvarado, and Angy Abreu and the Dominican Writers Association. Pa'lante!

Thank you to the various theatre communities (actors, designers, producers, directors and dramaturgs) from across the country who saw potential in the play City Without Altar and worked tirelessly to bring these words to life: Stages Repertory Theatre, Teatro Luna West, Milagro, Urban Theatre Company, the Ingenio Virtual Theatre Festival and the National New Play Network. In particular, a big shout out goes to Maya Malan-González, Alex Meda, José E. González, Trevor Boffone, Kenn McLaughlin, and Si'Mon Emmet for their dedication to putting Latinx stories on the stage.

Thank you to the scholars, academics and historians that have been telling this story long before me and who gave me some of their time and knowledge to help make this book possible. Edward Paulino, thank you for your work on uplifting and amplifying the stories of survivors and victims of the Haitian Massacre and for always checking in on me during this process and following my progress. Thank you for creating the Border of Lights organization to raise awareness on this piece of our shared history and inviting me to join you in the fight. May the work you are doing bring our island closer to finding peace and unity. Thank you to Dr. Lauren Derby for taking a chance and sharing interview transcripts and research with a no name poet who emailed you out of the blue one summer day back in 2015. These poems and this story would not exist without the interviews you and your colleagues conducted and were willing to share with me. I am forever indebted to your generosity and scholarship.

Thank you to every community that has cared for me over the years. This book and my work as a writer is only possible because of the many friends, family, caretakers, doctors and nurses that have kept me alive and stepped in to help when I was too stubborn or proud to ask for it myself.

Thank you to my in laws Pedro and Eucebia Mendez for having opened your home and your heart to me even when I struggle to be the perfect Dominican daughter-in-law.

Thank you Mami y Papi for bringing me into this world, allowing me to always believe in myself and for always being my biggest cheerleaders even if I have yet to be interviewed by Jorge Ramos. The stories I tell and the life I am able to lead are possible only because of you.

I would not be the woman or the writer I am today without the most important people: my partner in poetry and in life Lupe Mendez and our daughter Luz Maria. Everything I do, I do it for and because of you. I want you to be proud of me and I want our stories to live on long after I'm gone. Thank you for giving me a room of my own and for staying in bed late so I could use the early hours of the day to write in silence. Thank you for laughter and hugs and singing and dancing so I could find joy while writing these difficult poems. Thank you for making me slow down and surrender to whatever life may bring.

Last but most certainly not least I owe a debt of gratitude I may never be able to pay to all of the survivors of the Haitian Massacre who were willing to tell their stories. This book is dedicated and owed to them and to all those who did not make it and whose stories may never be known. I may never know all of your names but I have made a place for you on my altar and I will continue to share your story.

To support the ongoing work along the Dominican-Haitian border and in support of Haitian migrant rights both on the island and in the U.S.A, please consider following, supporting and donating to:

Roconoci.do

MUDHA (Movimiento de Mujeres Dominico-Hatiana)

Dominican@s por Derecho

Border of Lights

Haitian Bridge Alliance